# ALIENS

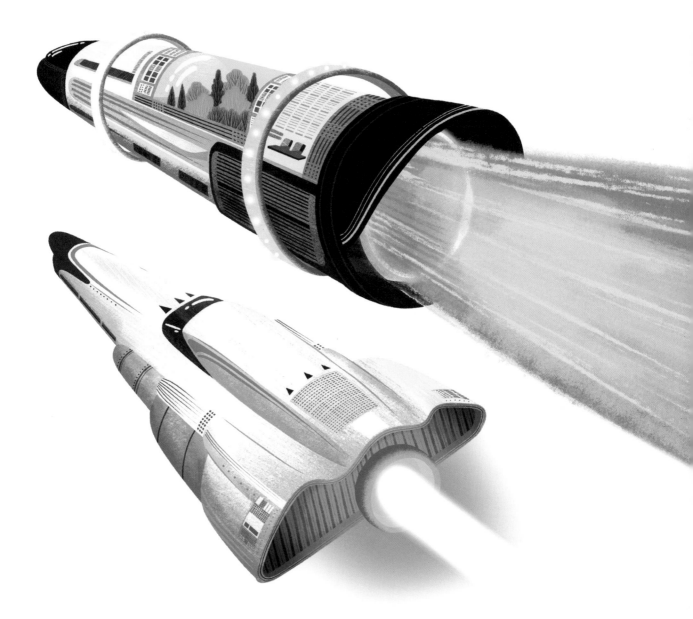

NEON SQUID

# CONTENTS

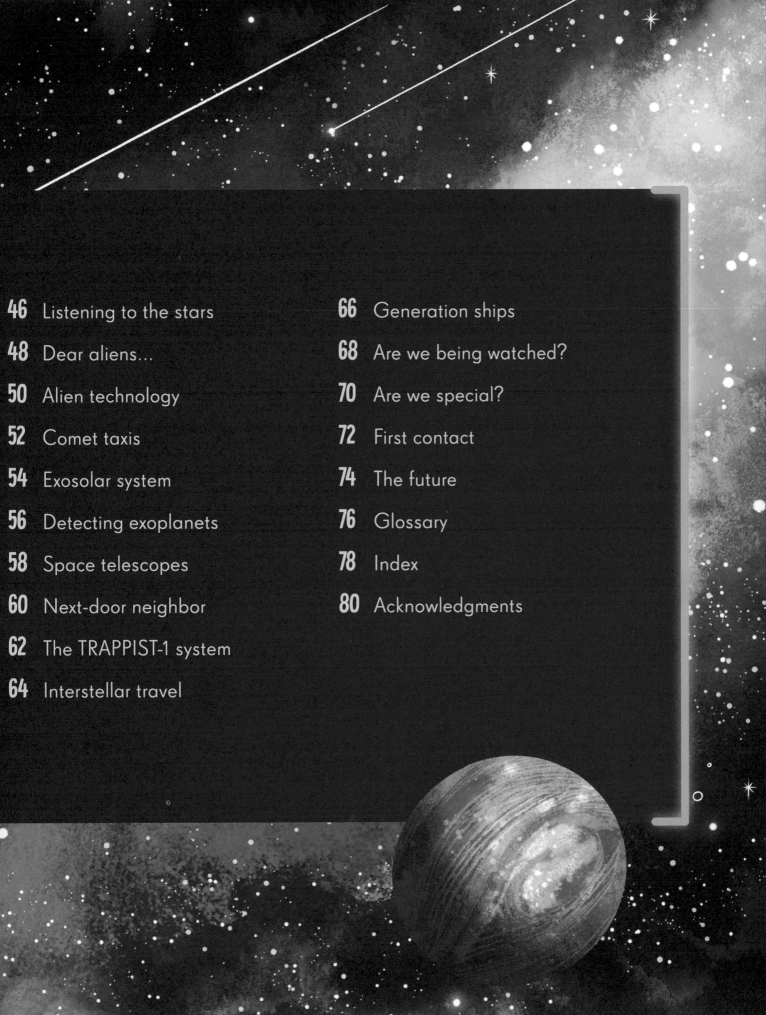

# THE ADVENTURE BEGINS

Welcome alien hunters, spacefarers, and curious souls! You might look at all of the amazing forms of life on Earth and wonder, does life exist elsewhere in the universe? Are we searching for this alien life, and will we ever find it? Will extraterrestrial life look like us or something beyond our wildest dreams?

In this book, I'll help you answer those questions by taking you across the solar system and deep into the cosmos. My name is Joalda and I'm someone just like you—I'm interested in life in the universe and helping humanity venture deeper into the unknown. I'm really excited to tell you all about the vast field of astrobiology, which is the study of life on Earth and in space, and show you how today's scientists are searching for aliens. Hold on tight because you're in for an out-of-this-world ride!

**Joalda Morancy**

THE ASTEROID BELT

THE SUN

VENUS

MARS

Ceres

EARTH

The moon

MERCURY

URANUS

THE KUIPER BELT

NEPTUNE

SATURN

Titan

Pluto

Enceladus

JUPITER

## ARE ALIENS NEARBY?

Extraterrestrials might be hiding in several places within our solar system! Our journey will start on Earth, where we'll analyze life here and the concept of aliens. We'll then venture to Venus, before heading to Mars and the asteroid belt. After that, we'll make a pit stop at one of Jupiter's moons, Europa, before exploring the worlds around Saturn. Then we'll speed past Uranus and Neptune and deep into the worlds beyond our cosmic neighborhood!

Europa

# IS THERE ANYONE OUT THERE?

## OUR PLACE IN SPACE

Placing ourselves on a celestial map can show how small we are in comparison to everything around us. When it comes to the grand scheme of things, we are just a tiny dot in the apparent nothingness of outer space.

**The universe**
Scientists think the universe was created in a huge explosion—the Big Bang. It is estimated that the universe contains more than 100 billion galaxies, each containing millions of stars and solar systems.

## THE DRAKE EQUATION

In 1961 an astrophysicist named Frank Drake developed an equation to try to work out the number of possible alien civilizations in the Milky Way galaxy. It was one of the first attempts at a scientific approach to searching for alien life. Though initially meant to be used only as an estimate, it has caused lots of arguments!

 **=** 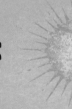 **X**

**Aliens**
Drake felt that the number of intelligent alien civilizations could be estimated by calculating the following...

**Stars**
First you need to know how often stars in the Milky Way form (which is at a rate of about 5–20 stars a year).

**Planets**
Then figure out how many stars have planets orbiting around them. Today we know most stars have a planet traveling around them.

The universe formed about 14 billion years ago, and, in case you hadn't noticed, it is HUGE. Not only that, but it's getting bigger—it continues to expand every second! As we try to understand its vastness, it makes us wonder: Where is everyone? Does life exist elsewhere, far out of reach? Surely we can't be the only living things in the universe. But... what if we are?

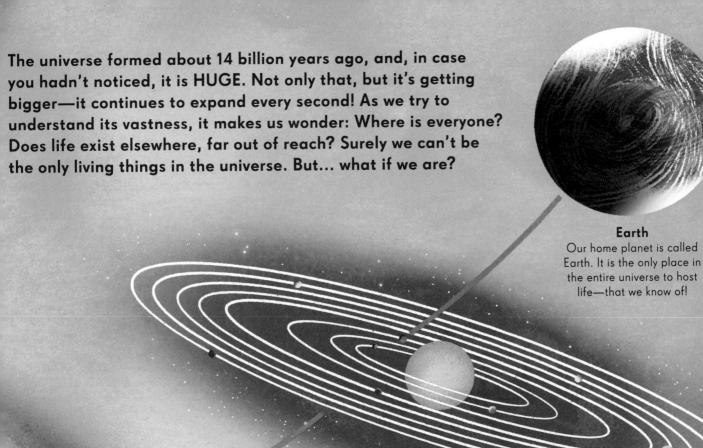

### Earth
Our home planet is called Earth. It is the only place in the entire universe to host life—that we know of!

### The Milky Way
We live within a constantly rotating spiral galaxy called the Milky Way. It is more than 100,000 light-years long, meaning it takes light that much time to travel across it! The Milky Way contains between 100 and 400 billion stars.

### The solar system
Our planet is in the solar system, a collection of planets, moons, and other celestial bodies that orbit (travel around) a star. Our star's name? You guessed it: the sun. The solar system is about 27,000 light-years away from the center of our galaxy.

 X  X  X  X

### Life-supporting planets
Then, out of all of the planets, estimate how many could be suitable places for life to form.

### Actual life
Then you take all of the planets we know for sure have life on them. At the moment there's only one: Earth!

### Intelligent life
Then you estimate how many planets that could support life (habitable planets) could develop intelligent life (like us).

### Communication
Then figure out how many of these smart aliens could create technology that could send a message to space.

### Time
Lastly, guess the number of years it will take an alien civilization to release signals into space.

# WATER WORLDS

## OCEAN WORLD

More than 70% of our planet's surface
is covered by liquid water. Most of it is
contained in our oceans.

One thing is usually a requirement when it comes to the search for life in the universe: liquid water. It is essential for all of the living things that we know exist. To understand water's role in our alien investigation, we need to know about Earth's history. How did our home planet transform from a hot ball of rock to the blue marble we know and love today? Let's rewind to 4.5 billion years ago.

# ASTEROID DELIVERY

We're still trying to understand where all of Earth's water came from. Most scientists think it was delivered to Earth a long time ago—during the solar system's formation.

**Protoplanetary disk**
The solar system started as a giant hot disk of gas and dust around the young sun. Slowly, the particles began to clump together to form planetesimals—early versions of today's planets.

**Asteroids**
Early Earth was bombarded with asteroids. One was so forceful that it created the moon! Many scientists believe that some of these asteroids contained the water that would one day fill our oceans.

**Volcanic activity**
Scientists believe that volcanoes also contributed to the formation of Earth's oceans. The volcanoes pumped out gases and water vapor, which turned to liquid water as Earth's surface cooled.

# THE GOLDILOCKS ZONE

Liquid water can only exist in certain conditions. If it's too hot it evaporates, and if it's too cold it freezes. Scientists always first look for alien life in a solar system's "habitable zone," also known as "the Goldilocks Zone." In this area, the temperatures are just right for water to exist in liquid form. It's named after the fairy-tale character Goldilocks, who didn't like her porridge too hot or too cold.

The Goldilocks Zone

## SINGLE-CELLED ORGANISMS

Cells are the building blocks of life—you're made up of trillions of them! The smallest known forms of life are made up of just one cell. These are called single-celled organisms, and they were the first life-forms to emerge on Earth.

Plants

## PLANTS

Plants are made up of lots of cells. They cover the Earth, with more than 400,000 species existing! They are an essential part of the environment, providing oxygen and serving as food and homes for many types of animals.

## VERTEBRATES

Animals can be split into two types: vertabrates and invertebrates. Vertebrates have a backbone and internal skeleton. They include fish, birds, reptiles, amphibians, and mammals. The first vertebrates formed more than 500 million years ago. Some vertebrates have evolved into intelligent beings—that's right, humans!

# THE ORIGINS OF LIFE

Animals

Understanding how life first evolved on Earth can give us clues for what to search for when we're alien hunting. Biologists estimate that 3.8 billion years ago, a chemical soup in Earth's oceans created the first simple life-forms. These organisms were powered by sunlight—using a process called photosynthesis to produce oxygen. Gradually, as oxygen levels on the planet increased, more complex life was able to develop. This family tree shows how all life-forms on Earth are linked.

## INVERTEBRATES

Invertebrates lack a backbone and internal skeleton. There are many more invertebrates on Earth than vertebrates—mostly insects! Some invertebrates have an exoskeleton covering the outside of their body. Exoskeletons can be tough, such as a crab's shell, or soft, like a jellyfish. The first invertebrates appeared sometime between 1 billion and 650 million years ago.

## LAYERS OF TIME

We can learn more about the history of life on Earth by studying fossils. Over time, minerals form layers of rock on top of dead organisms. Based on the location of the rock layer, scientists can date the fossils and understand how life evolved.

# UFO SPOTTING

An unidentified flying object, or UFO, is the term we use for anything that whizzes through the sky that we can't explain. Humans have been recording UFO sightings from as early as 240 BCE, when ancient Chinese astronomers noted what turned out to be a passing comet. Even though we associate the word with aliens, a UFO can be anything—from a birthday-party balloon floating off in the distance to a rocket blasting into space.

## BLURRY PHOTOS

Unfortunately it's hard to predict when a UFO might go speeding by! As a result lots of the photos that exist of UFOs are very blurry or difficult to make sense of. This questionable evidence leads many to presume the photos are fake.

## ABDUCTIONS

A common misconception is that UFOs are flying saucers that come in the middle of the night to abduct living things, from humans to cows! There is absolutely no evidence that this has ever happened. But the stories make good movies!

# CONSPIRACY THEORIES

As more and more UFO sightings occur, people come up with their own theories about what's behind the strange events. Many believe that various governments have knowledge about alien visitors and are in constant communication with extraterrestrials. Before believing one of these conspiracy theories, it is important to analyze all of the evidence. Most UFO sightings have a reasonable, non-alien explanation!

**FLYING SAUCER DISCOVERED?**

**Headline news**
The local newspaper reported all of the various times the air force changed its story. The public couldn't get enough of the scandal, and conspiracy theories continue to this day.

## THE ROSWELL INCIDENT

One of the most famous UFO conspiracy theories surrounds the Roswell incident of 1947 in New Mexico. A rancher found a mysterious wreckage on his property and believed it could be from a UFO. He called a sheriff to investigate, who reported it to the United States Air Force. The air force first claimed they'd found a flying saucer, before stating that the wreckage was from a weather balloon. Eventually it was revealed to be spy equipment from a top-secret testing program! Safe to say, the public was suspicious of the entire situation.

# AREA 51

Area 51 is a highly classified air-force base in Nevada. Due to the secretive nature of what goes on at the base, many conspiracy theories have formed. Some people believe that UFOs and extraterrestrials are being kept from the public eye. Others have reported strange sightings in the skies, and retired military members have claimed to have seen alien technology inside Area 51! Despite all of the rumors, we have yet to see any concrete evidence of aliens.

**What's really going on?**
Area 51 is actually a base for the development and testing of advanced aircraft, which explains the weird sightings in the sky!

**Security**
Fencing around Area 51 warns potential trespassers to stay away and not take any photos.

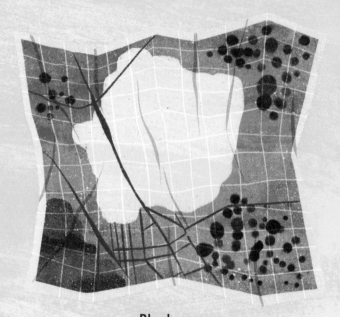

**Blank map**
Until the government publically recognized Area 51's existence in 2013, people didn't know exactly what was there.

# LITTLE GREEN MEN

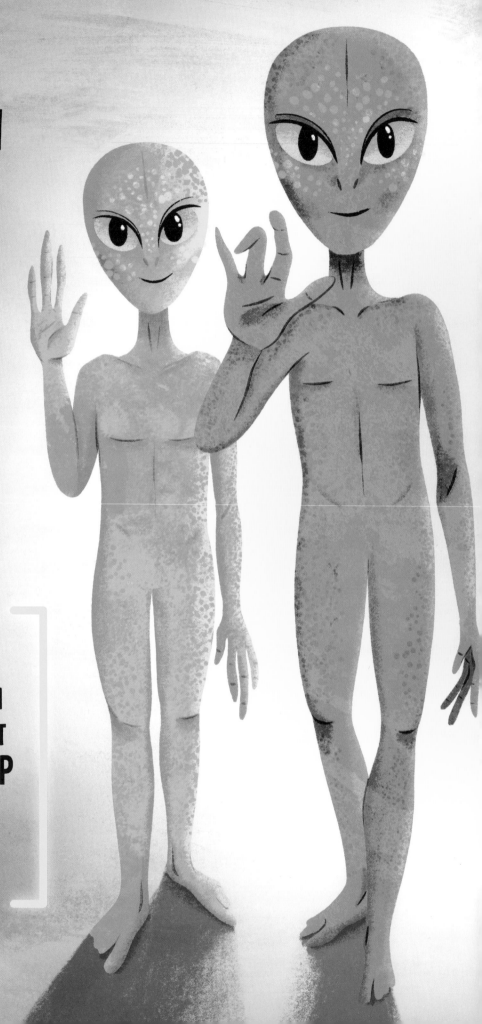

## CLASSIC ALIENS

The classic idea of an alien has a head, a neck, a torso, two arms, and two legs... Wait a minute. Does that sound familiar to you? We're describing a human body! But the fact is that aliens could look like anything. We humans look the way we do because we have evolved that way to live on Earth. On an alien planet, life could be wildly different!

"THIRTEEN **LITTLE GREEN MEN** FROM MERCURY STEPPED OUT OF THEIR **SPACE SHIP** FOR A VISIT."

*The Corpus Christi Times*
newspaper, November 1, 1938

When someone says the word *alien* to you, the first images that appear in your brain are probably green creatures with deep black marbles for eyes. Am I right? This idea of aliens has been popular since the early 20th century. One of the first recorded instances of the term *little green men* was in a 1938 issue of *The Corpus Christi Times* in Texas. The newspaper recounted the panic that followed a Halloween radio broadcast of a book called *The War of the Worlds*, which focuses on an alien invasion. Unfortunately some of the listeners had thought it was real!

## GREEN MEN EVERYWHERE

Early alien films and comics were full of little green men. Over time this has changed, and modern depictions of aliens are much more vaired. Even though we may laugh at the idea of little green men today, we can still see the impact and significance of this idea—just look at Yoda from the *Star Wars* movies!

### Television shows
If you ever come across TV shows from the 60s and 70s, you'll notice a tendency for little green men to crop up. Even today the expression "little green men" is associated with aliens.

### Comics
In the first half of the 20th century comics were full of little green men coming to Earth. Generations of kids presumed all aliens were green.

# A HELLISH WORLD

The planet Venus was once a world similar to Earth, with oceans scattered across its surface. There is a possibility that alien life was once present— maybe tiny organisms going about their lives in the Venusian seas? However, Venus is much closer to the sun than we are on Earth. As the solar system formed, the sun got brighter and hotter. What was once a wet world has now become a baking hot, dry, inhospitable rock.

## TRAPPED HEAT

How did Venus become the hottest planet in the solar system, with surface temperatures over 850°F (450°C)? Well, incoming radiation from the sun was trapped within the atmosphere, increasing temperatures and evaporating Venus's oceans. This is called the runaway greenhouse effect.

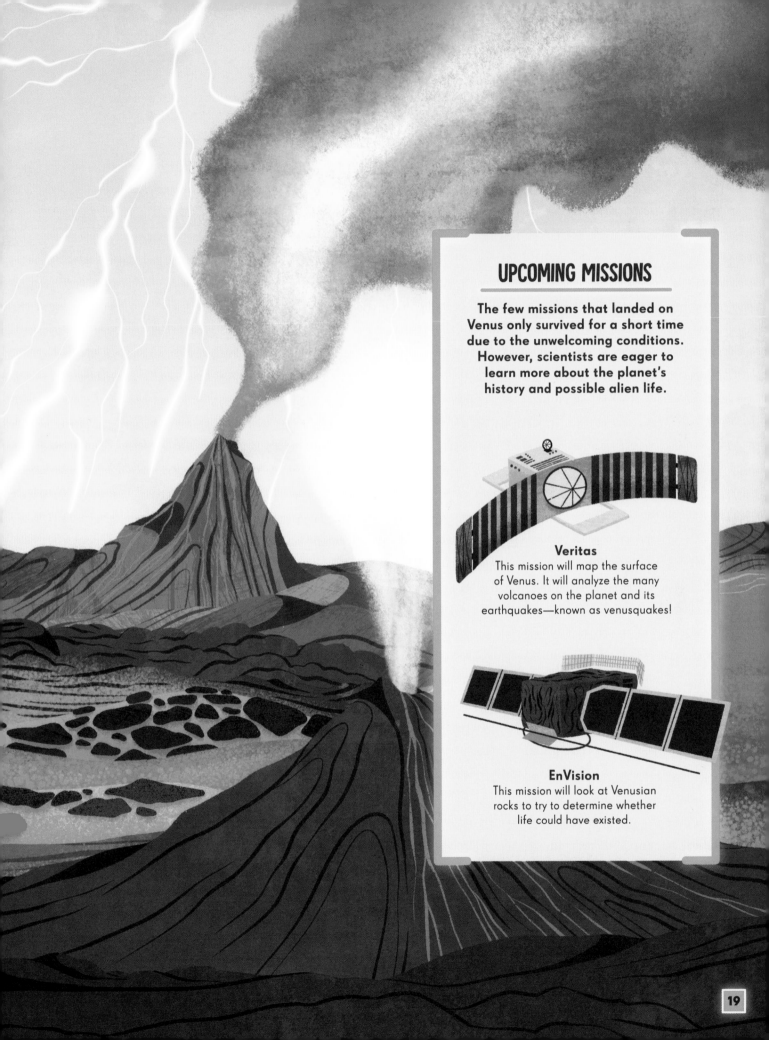

## UPCOMING MISSIONS

The few missions that landed on Venus only survived for a short time due to the unwelcoming conditions. However, scientists are eager to learn more about the planet's history and possible alien life.

### Veritas

This mission will map the surface of Venus. It will analyze the many volcanoes on the planet and its earthquakes—known as venusquakes!

### EnVision

This mission will look at Venusian rocks to try to determine whether life could have existed.

# THE CLOUDS OF VENUS

Scientists aren't looking for signs of life on the surface of Venus—the extreme temperatures and high pressure mean it is highly unlikely to survive there. But up in the clouds is a different story. Within the thick atmosphere of Venus exists a more gentle environment that may be hiding aliens. The Venusian clouds may be home to extremophiles—tough, tiny organisms capable of withstanding the harsh conditions.

## DAVINCI+

After the possible discovery of phospine on Venus (see top right), NASA decided to send missions to the planet to investigate. DAVINCI+ is a robotic probe that will take measurements of the Venusian atmosphere.

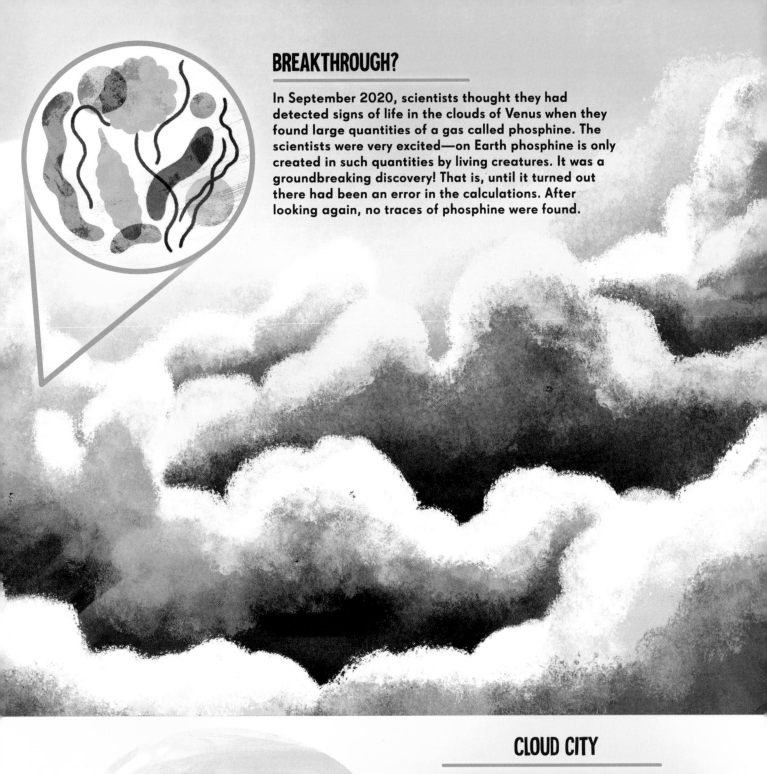

## BREAKTHROUGH?

In September 2020, scientists thought they had detected signs of life in the clouds of Venus when they found large quantities of a gas called phosphine. The scientists were very excited—on Earth phosphine is only created in such quantities by living creatures. It was a groundbreaking discovery! That is, until it turned out there had been an error in the calculations. After looking again, no traces of phosphine were found.

## CLOUD CITY

One day in the future, building cities within the clouds of Venus could help scientists studying the planet's atmosphere. Aerostats—aircraft lighter than air—could float high in the atmosphere, and the clouds would protect humans from space radiation.

# A HISTORY OF MARS

Mars is named after the Roman god of war. It is the fourth planet from the sun in the solar system and formed around the same time as Earth, though it ended up half the size and with a third of its gravity (meaning you can jump really high on the surface!). Though the two planets have many differences, there are also similarities. For example a day on Mars (called a Sol) is about the same length as one on Earth. Another similarity is that at some point in its history, Mars had flowing oceans that may have harbored alien life.

## MARS TODAY

The red planet is no longer covered in gushing rivers. Instead the planet is dry and dusty, its color coming from the rust that covers its surface. Mars is home to the tallest volcano mountain in the solar system, Olympus Mons, and one of the deepest canyons, Valles Marineris. It has an extremely thin atmosphere that is less than 1% of the thickness of Earth's. Mars is a barren rock seemingly void of life... or is it?

## MARTIAN MOONS

Orbiting Mars are its two moons, Phobos and Deimos, named after the twin sons of Ares – the ancient Greek equivalent of Mars. These two irregularly shaped rocks have unknown origins. One theory is that they were once asteroids captured by Mars, while another thinks they formed after something collided with the planet.

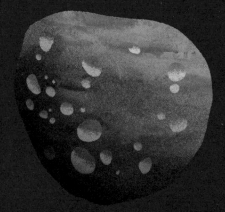

**Phobos**
Each century, Phobos gets a little closer to Mars, meaning one day it may spectacularly crash into Mars!

**Deimos**
Deimos is about half the size of Phobos, and it's much farther away from Mars.

## WET SURFACE

Mars's history as a water world makes it a prime candidate in the ongoing search for life in the universe. Even though we might not see living organisms today, we can study areas that used to hold water for signs of life. You might be wondering, where did the water go? Well, billions of years ago Mars lost its magnetic field, which protected it from harmful particles from the sun called solar wind. The solar wind stripped away the Martian atmosphere. A thin atmosphere doesn't allow liquid water to exist, though frozen water can still be found at the planet's poles.

## JEZERO CRATER

NASA's Mars rover, Perseverance, is exploring Jezero Crater on Mars. This crater was once a lake. Some of the rocks here are 3.6 billion years old. It's an excellent spot to learn if anything once survived in the Martian lake.

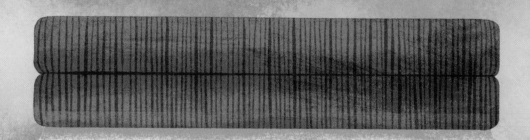

# WHAT'S INSIDE?

Scientists need lots of materials in order to mimic Mars. The first ingredients are the gases carbon dioxide and nitrogen, which is what the thin Martian atmosphere is mostly made of. Next, they need to re-create Martian soil. Last they'll add tiny microbes that will act as their test subjects. By studying how they react to the environment the scientists will get a better idea of what life-forms could survive on Mars.

# MARS JARS

The first space biology experiments to exist were Mars Jars. These simple containers were a smart way for scientists to experiment with how tiny organisms (microbes) from Earth interacted in a simulated Martian environment. The jars were kind of like terrariums you put plants in. Today, Mars Jars have evolved into larger chambers that allow scientists to re-create conditions on Mars, with the ability to adjust the temperature or atmosphere if necessary. This allows them to perform in-depth experiments concerning Martian life.

**1950s experiments**
The first Mars Jar was invented in the kitchen of a professor's home in 1953. Many more followed in labs in the following years.

# VIKING **RAID**

The Viking program was NASA's first successful attempt at landing a spacecraft on Mars. NASA was looking for signs of life on the planet, also known as biosignatures. It was a groundbreaking moment for the field of astrobiology! Launching in 1975 and arriving in 1976, the two Viking spacecraft were able to take photos of the planet and perform experiments.

## ORBITER AND LANDER

The Viking spacecraft consisted of two parts: an orbiter that circled the planet and a lander that went to the surface. The orbiter took photos and played a crucial role in determining where the lander would touch down.

## PARACHUTING DOWN

When the lander was almost at the surface a parachute was deployed to slow it down. The spacecraft needed to be in one piece once it made it to the Martian surface!

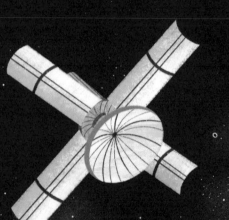

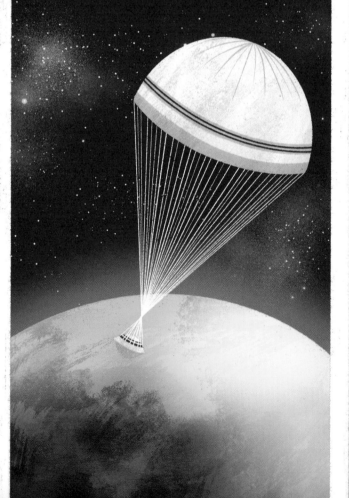

## ON THE SURFACE

The Viking 1 lander took the first image of the Martian surface, a monumental moment in space-exploration history. The next task was to study the biology of Mars by looking at the soil. The hope was that these experiments would indicate the presence of life, but the results said otherwise.

## HIT THE BURNERS

For the last stage of the journey the lander separated from the parachute. To lose even more speed, it fired three tiny engines that slowed down the spacecraft.

# SEARCHING FOR MARTIANS

## PERSEVERANCE ROVER

NASA's Perseverance rover touched down on Mars in 2021. Its mission? To look for hints of ancient life and to store rock samples to send back to scientists on Earth. Perseverance is currently situated in Jezero Crater, which was once a lake and river delta.

**1 Supercam**
This piece of equipment shoots lasers at Martian rocks to study what they're made of.

**2 MastCam-Z**
Acting as the main eyes of Perseverance, MastCam-Z can take high-definition 3D images.

**3 MEDA**
This weather station measures wind speed and direction, humidity, temperature, and pressure.

**4 RIMFAX**
This radar scans below the Martian surface. It's the first of its kind sent to Mars!

## CHOPPER ASSISTANT

The Ingenuity helicopter is Perseverance's partner in crime. During its journey to Mars, Ingenuity was tucked away in the rover's belly. A couple of months after landing on Mars it took flight for the first time. Ingenuity is meant to help engineers understand how flight works on another planet. Because the Martian atmosphere is so thin, the helicopter has to be extremely lightweight and powerful. Learning this technology will pave the way for future scientific missions!

One way to explore Mars is through rovers—robots that send information about the Red Planet back to Earth. These rovers can work in inhospitable places humans can't yet set foot in and perform useful experiments. There have been numerous rover missions, and there are more to come. Robots have taken over the entire planet! In the past, missions tried to find out why the planet was barren and seemingly lifeless. Today, Martian rovers are searching for signs of past life.

**5 MOXIE**
This tool helps us learn how to produce oxygen on Mars (useful for rocket fuel and breathing).

**6 SHERLOC & WATSON**
These two instruments work together to look for signs of life inside Martian rocks.

**7 PIXL**
This scans rocks using X-rays. It is able to see things as small as a grain of sand!

**8 Rover wheels**
Perseverance has six sturdy titanium wheels, each with its own motor.

# HUMANITY ON MARS

A human mission to Mars may sound like something from a sci-fi film, but today scientists and engineers are trying to make it a reality. The robots that currently inhabit the red planet are doing a fantastic job learning more about Martian history, but the truth is that humans on the ground could significantly speed up the search for life on Mars. The current goal is for the first crewed Mars mission to land sometime in the 2030s.

A trip to Mars won't be a one-way ticket! We'll need to design a rocket that can bring astronauts home safely too.

Like the robots, astronauts will be eager to look inside Martian rocks.

## A HARD DAY'S WORK

A trip to Mars won't just be an out-of-this-world vacation. An astronaut crew will be working hard, performing experiments every day. They'll have the entire science community on Earth awaiting their results!

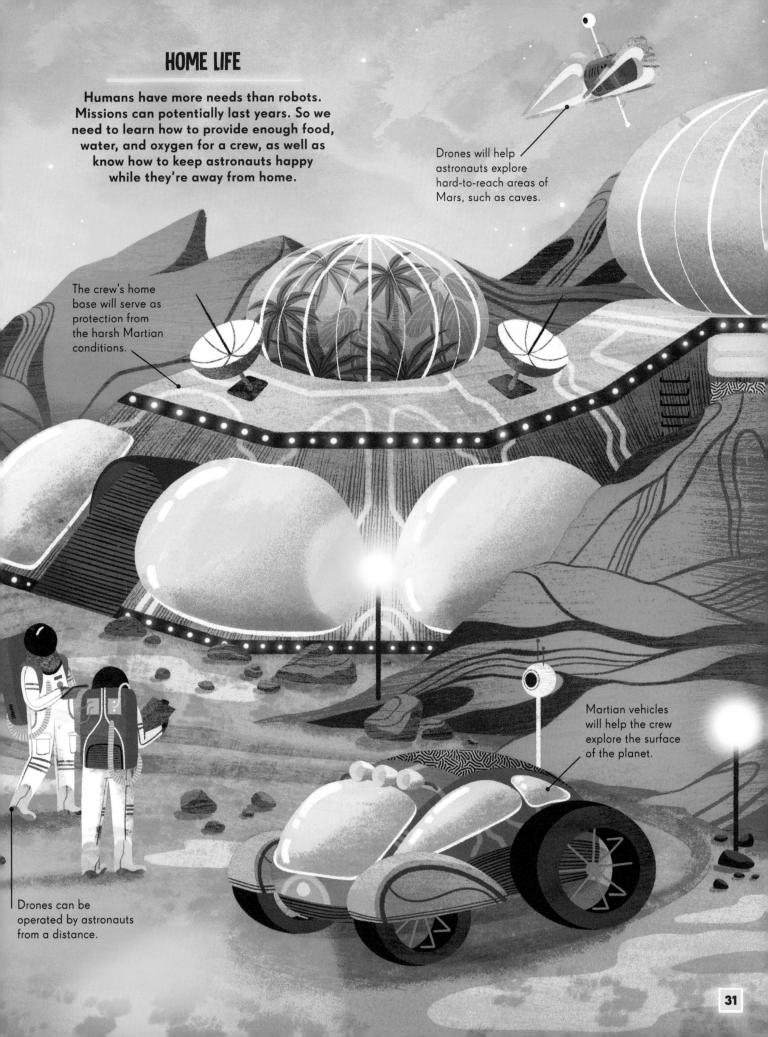

# HOME LIFE

Humans have more needs than robots. Missions can potentially last years. So we need to learn how to provide enough food, water, and oxygen for a crew, as well as know how to keep astronauts happy while they're away from home.

Drones will help astronauts explore hard-to-reach areas of Mars, such as caves.

The crew's home base will serve as protection from the harsh Martian conditions.

Martian vehicles will help the crew explore the surface of the planet.

Drones can be operated by astronauts from a distance.

# CERES

Deep within the asteroid belt lies the dwarf planet Ceres. After Earth, it holds the most water in the solar system, and scientists wonder if it has an underground ocean. Could Ceres be home to alien life?

## DWARF PLANET

Scientists classified Ceres as a planet when it was discovered in 1801. This stuck for half a century, until it was reclassified as an asteroid. In 2006, scientists changed their minds again, deciding that due to its large size Ceres was a dwarf planet.

# THE ASTEROID BELT

The asteroid belt sits between the orbits of Mars and Jupiter. It is home to many asteroids that contain lots of water. Once upon a time these pieces of rock may have brought water to Earth, possibly sparking the start of life here. This means studying the asteroid belt is important for understanding how we came into existence.

The asteroid belt

## MISSION TO CERES

In 2015 NASA's Dawn probe became the first spacecraft to visit Ceres. While there, it detected a thin atmosphere made of water vapor. Scientists believe this atmosphere was created by icy volcanoes erupting water and ice from the surface. Dawn didn't detect any signs of life while it orbited Ceres.

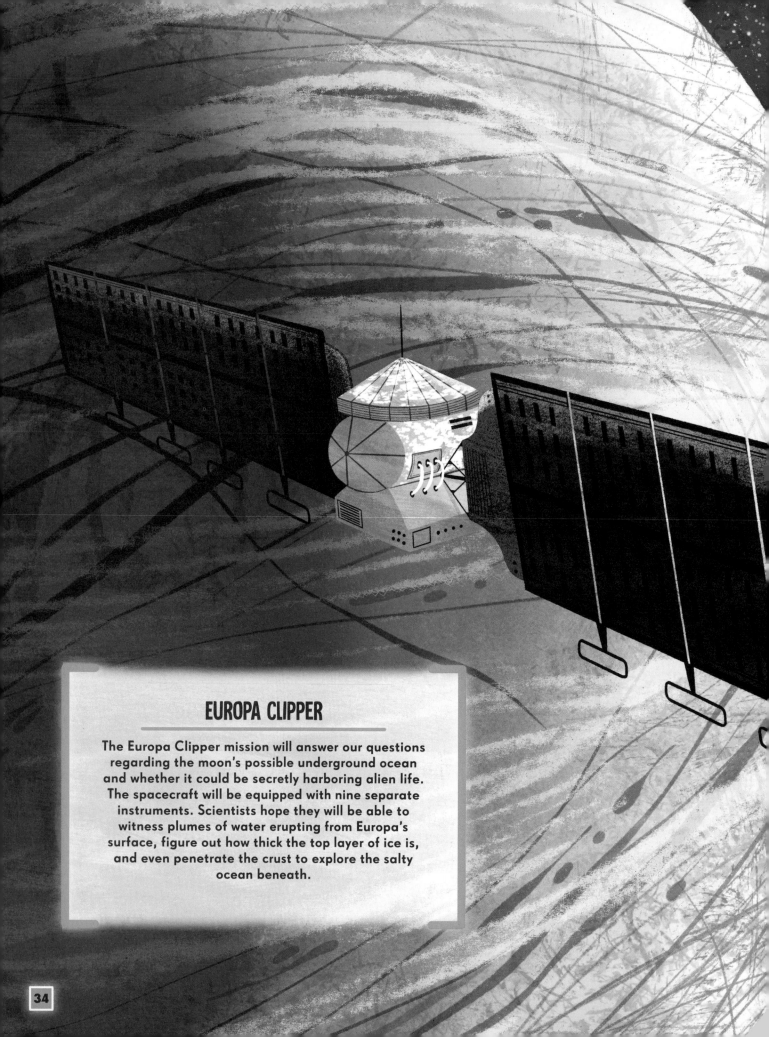

# EUROPA CLIPPER

The Europa Clipper mission will answer our questions regarding the moon's possible underground ocean and whether it could be secretly harboring alien life. The spacecraft will be equipped with nine separate instruments. Scientists hope they will be able to witness plumes of water erupting from Europa's surface, figure out how thick the top layer of ice is, and even penetrate the crust to explore the salty ocean beneath.

# THE FROZEN WORLD OF EUROPA

As we continue our search for life, we arrive at huge planets made of gas—the gas giants. First up is the largest planet in the solar system, Jupiter. Hurtling around it every three and a half days is the moon Europa. At first glance, Europa looks like nothing more than a scratched ball of ice, though it may be hiding something underneath its hard surface...

Because it's so close to Jupiter, Europa is constantly being affected by the large planet's gravity. Europa literally squishes smaller when it gets close to the planet, before reverting to normal as it moves away again. These changes generate heat inside the moon. This warmth melts the ice— meaning there may be a liquid ocean hidden beneath Europa's icy surface!

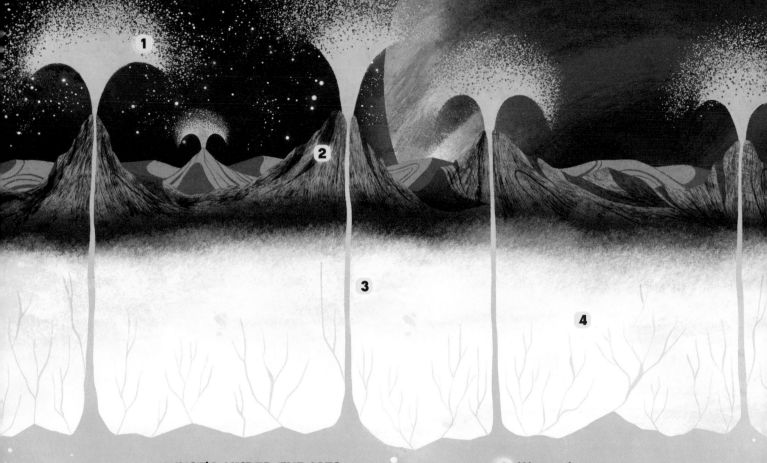

# WHAT'S UNDER THE ICE?

Scientists expect the ocean on Europa to contain twice as much water as Earth's oceans! Even though the actual contents of the sea remain unknown, scientists predict it will be a deep ocean with a rocky seabed. Their biggest hope is to discover a tiny speck of life. A single microorganism could be enough to solve the age-old question: Are we alone in the universe?

**1 Water plumes**
The Hubble Space Telescope has spotted possible geysers of water spouting from Europa. If they exist, we can study the moon's ocean without digging through the icy crust.

**2 Icy volcanoes**
Instead of spewing out hot lava, volcanoes on Europa might shoot water vapor into the sky! Volcanoes like this are called cryovolcanoes.

**3 Narrow passageways**
Pressure from under the icy shell probably creates cracks in it. This leads to water traveling up the narrow fissures to the surface.

**4 Thick ice crust**
The layer of crust is estimated to be anywhere between 9–16 miles (15–25 km) thick, about two to three times the height of Mount Everest.

**5 Deep, deep sea**
Europa's ocean is thought to be about ten times deeper than the deepest point of Earth's oceans.

## HYDROTHERMAL VENTS

Europa is believed to have two things essential for life to exist: water and organic chemicals. The last thing needed is an energy source organisms can feed on, and underwater volcanoes called hydrothermal vents can supply them. These structures spew out heat and water streams full of nutrients. We've seen life on Earth flourish in these hot environments, so scientists hope to see something similar on Europa!

## ALIEN LIFE

Scientists expect any aliens living in Europa's ocean to be tiny microorganisms, but more complex life may have evolved. These aliens could be bioluminescent, producing their own light in the darkness. Or maybe they use sound to navigate their surroundings, similar to dolphins. The possibilities are endless, and life on Europa could be wildly different from what we have imagined!

# THE MYSTERIES OF TITAN

Titan is a moon of the ringed gas giant Saturn, and it's like no other in our cosmic neighborhood. It is the only known moon with a substantial atmosphere, a golden haze comprised mostly of the gas nitrogen—just like Earth. Planetary scientists believe that Titan is hiding an ocean of water beneath its surface (you may have noticed this is a common theme!). One of the most exciting things about Titan is that it is the only other place in the solar system that has lakes, rivers, and seas.

## UNUSUAL LAKES

The Cassini-Huygens space probe detected various bodies of liquid on Titan's surface. Instead of water, these lakes and seas were formed of liquid methane and ethane. Some of the largest seas are at least a thousand feet deep and could contain alien organisms! All life as we know it is water-based, but what we discover on Titan may change this idea.

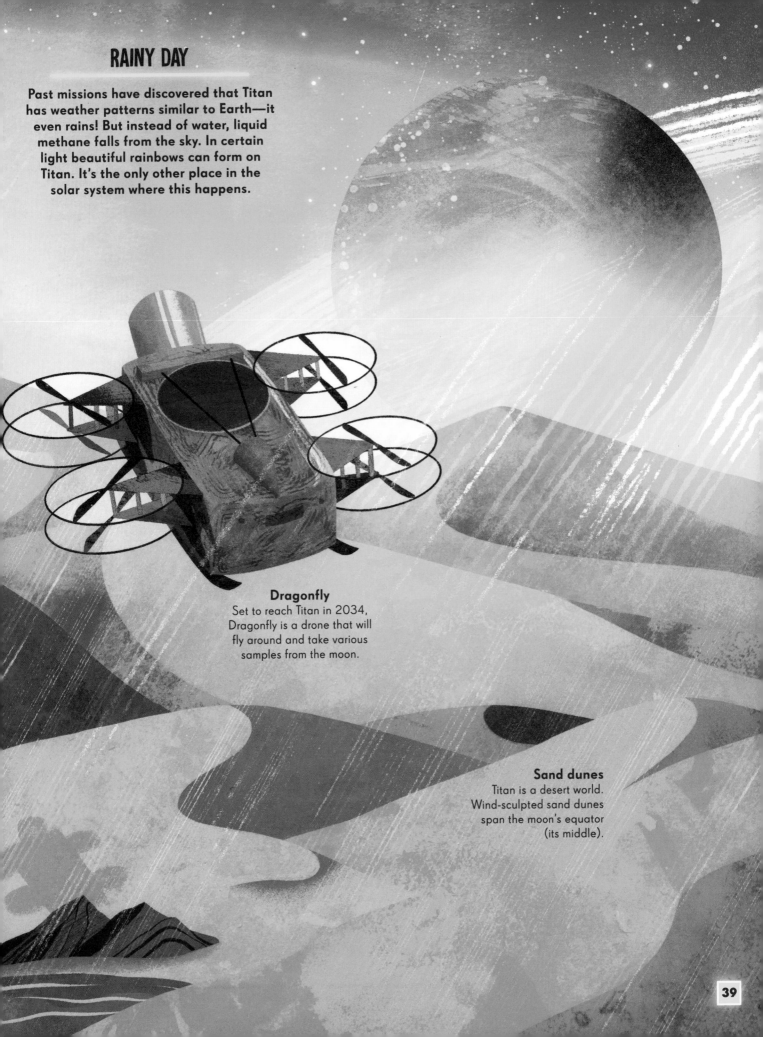

# RAINY DAY

Past missions have discovered that Titan has weather patterns similar to Earth—it even rains! But instead of water, liquid methane falls from the sky. In certain light beautiful rainbows can form on Titan. It's the only other place in the solar system where this happens.

**Dragonfly**
Set to reach Titan in 2034, Dragonfly is a drone that will fly around and take various samples from the moon.

**Sand dunes**
Titan is a desert world. Wind-sculpted sand dunes span the moon's equator (its middle).

# A TRIP TO ENCELADUS

Enceladus is a tiny moon that looks innocent at first glance. Orbiting Saturn, it's like any other celestial body—smothered in craters and fissures. But once you start to dive deeper, you realize that the icy moon is a fantastic candidate in our search for life in the solar system. In 2005 the Cassini spacecraft swung by the moon, witnessing volcanoes spewing out liquid and ice. Cassini flew through these icy volcano plumes and detected loads of organic molecules—the building blocks necessary for life. As a result, Enceladus is a fan favorite among alien hunters.

**Frozen moon**
Due to its frozen white surface, Enceladus reflects about 90% of sunlight, making it one of the brightest objects in the solar system. The surface is very, very cold.

## RING BUILDER

One of the most iconic features of Saturn is its majestic rings, which are made up of chunks of ice and rock. The ice volcanoes on Enceladus shoot out material that helps build one of Saturn's rings—the E ring. By studying the E ring, we can learn more about the salty ocean within Enceladus.

## UNDERGROUND OCEAN

Similar to Europa, scientists believe that an underground ocean exists within Enceladus. While traveling through Saturn's E ring, Cassini detected tiny particles of something called silica. This discovery led scientists to believe that hydrothermal vents exist at the bottom of Enceladus's seafloor. These vents could provide the energy alien life needs to survive. Because the moon's thick icy shell prevents sunlight from reaching the ocean, aliens on Enceladus may be blind.

### Makemake
This is the second-brightest dwarf planet in the Kuiper belt.

### Eris
Eris is the biggest dwarf planet we've found so far. Its large size led scientists to believe that it was the solar system's tenth planet.

# BEYOND NEPTUNE

### Pluto
The most famous object in the Kuiper belt! Pluto's heart was crushed after scientists demoted it from a planet to a dwarf planet.

### Quaoar
Scientists have detected water ice on the surface of Quaoar, possibly the result of cryovolcanoes.

## DISTANT NEIGHBORHOOD

The doughnut-shaped Kuiper belt begins at about 30 astronomical units (AU) from the sun—one AU being the distance between the Earth and the sun. The objects within this distant region are thought to be leftovers from the solar system's formation. Planetary scientists have found Kuiper belt–like disks around other stars in our galaxy.

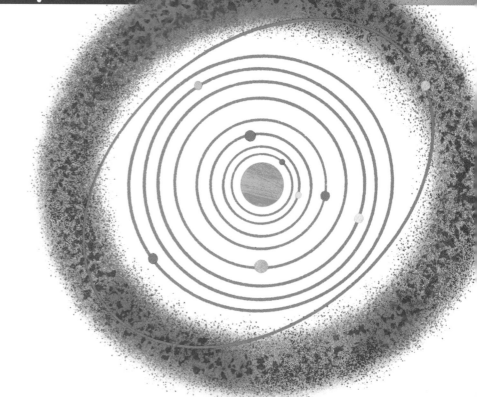

The solar system doesn't just end with Neptune! There are tons of celestial objects that orbit in a space called the Kuiper belt, including asteroids, comets, and icy bodies. Some bodies, called Trans-Neptunian Objects (TNOs), exist beyond this area. Asteroids and comets from beyond Neptune may have collided with Earth early in its history, providing the ingredients necessary for life to evolve.

### Orcus
Orcus is a Trans-Neptunian Object with its own moon called Vanth.

### Haumea
This dwarf planet spins on its axis very quickly, distorting its shape and making the planet oval-shaped.

### Sedna
This distant body takes over 11,400 years to complete a single orbit of the sun.

## NEW HORIZONS

New Horizons was the first spacecraft sent to study Pluto and other objects in the Kuiper belt. It launched in 2006 and reached Pluto almost a decade later. New Horizons provided groundbreaking information on Pluto, including the possibility of an underground ocean that could host alien life (another one!). Now it is traveling deeper into the Kuiper belt, studying distant objects that have never been looked at before.

# THE ARECIBO MESSAGE

In 1974, scientists decided it was about time we tried
to make contact with aliens. They carefully created
something called the Arecibo message and broadcasted
it into space. The message contained information about
life on Earth for any aliens that might hear it.
We haven't received a response... yet!

## THE DISH

The Arecibo Telescope was located in
a sinkhole in Puerto Rico. It was one
of the world's largest radio telescopes,
contributing to years of astronomical
discoveries. After decades of service,
the dish collapsed in 2020.

## THE DESTINATION

The Arecibo message was sent to a cluster of stars located in the Hercules constellation, over 22,000 light-years away. The message is traveling at about the speed of light, meaning it will take about 22,000 years to reach the star cluster.

# THE MESSAGE

**The message was designed by famous astrophysicists including Francis Drake and Carl Sagan. The radio signal can be separated into parts that explain humanity, our place in the universe, and chemical elements found on Earth. The message is broken down below (hopefully aliens can understand it).**

**1 Numbers**
This section describes how we count! Astrophysicists depicted the numbers one to ten.

**2 Elements**
The elements hydrogen, carbon, nitrogen, oxygen, and phosphorus are represented here. These help form DNA, the basis for all life on Earth.

**3 DNA**
This represents the building blocks that make up our DNA.

**4 Double helix**
This is the shape of our DNA.

**5 Humans!**
Here is a stick person! The 1974 population of Earth is to the left, and on the right is the average height of a human.

**6 Solar system**
Next, we have a diagram of the solar system, with the position of Earth marked. Underneath is the Arecibo Telescope.

# LISTENING TO THE STARS

## VERY LARGE ARRAY

The Very Large Array (VLA) is an observatory located in New Mexico. It consists of 28 radio telescopes that are arranged in a Y-shape. The SETI Institute teamed up with the VLA in 2020 to collaborate on alien hunting research.

### Mix and match
The different antennae can be moved if needed. Transporters pick up the antennae and use railroad lines to move them to new positions!

There are many groups of scientists who dedicate time and research to looking for alien civilizations. The Search for Extraterrestrial Intelligence (SETI) Institute uses special radio telescopes to send messages out into the stars and listen for any incoming radio signals. Scientists believe that since human technology produces a lot of radio signals, alien technology might be doing the same thing!

# ALLEN TELESCOPE ARRAY

The Allen Telescope Array (ATA) is a set of 42 radio telescopes specially designed for SETI research, the first of its kind! It's located in California.

## Getting bigger

The ATA was initially planned to be developed in four stages, starting with 42 telescopes and slowly scaling up until it reaches an array of 350 telescopes. However funding has proved to be a problem!

# DEAR ALIENS...

Humans are curious when it comes to alien life. We will do whatever we can to make contact with strangers in the cosmos, including sending messages that could help aliens understand what life on Earth is like! The first messages were sent with the Pioneer missions of the 1970s. The idea then expanded into an even larger project with the Voyager missions and their famous Golden Record.

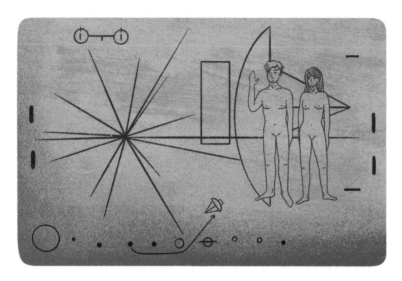

## PIONEER PLAQUE

The Pioneer missions were the first that were planned to leave the solar system. Since they were venturing into the unknown, scientists decided to place a plaque on board the spacecraft in case any intelligent life came across it. The golden plaque included drawings of a human man and woman, a chemical diagram, information about the solar system, and the planned route of the Pioneer spacecraft.

## VOYAGER MISSIONS

The two Voyager spacecraft explored parts of our solar system, such as Uranus and Neptune, for the first time. They were also the first spacecraft to enter interstellar space—the area beyond the solar system. Voyager 1 and 2 launched a couple of months apart in 1977 and are still transmitting data back to Earth to this day, despite being billions of miles away! Even though the Voyager missions are expected to stop being operational in 2025, when they can no longer power their electronic instruments, the spacecraft will continue to travel the Milky Way for thousands of years to come.

**A long journey**
Voyager 1 and Voyager 2 were sent to learn more about gas giants Jupiter and Saturn. Voyager 2 also traveled to the ice giants Uranus and Neptune.

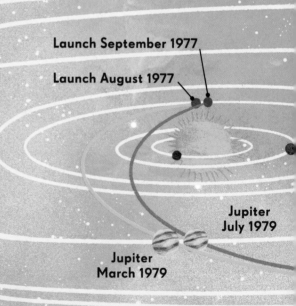

Launch September 1977

Launch August 1977

Jupiter July 1979

Jupiter March 1979

## Golden Record

On board each Voyager spacecraft was a Golden Record that told the story of humankind. They contained images of day-to-day life, various sounds (examples on the right), and spoken greetings in 55 different languages.

**Crickets and frogs**

**Elephant, hyena, bird**

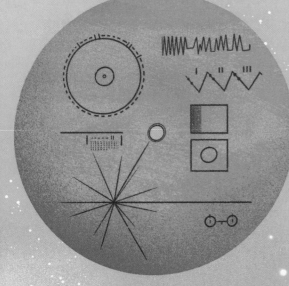

**Tractor**

**Orchestra**

**Voyager 1**

**Voyager 2**

**Neptune
August 1989**

**Uranus
January 1986**

**Saturn
August 1981**

**Saturn
November 1980**

# ALIEN
# TECHNOLOGY

If you don't have time to wait for aliens to reply to your messages, you'll be relieved to hear there may be other ways to find extraterrestrial civilizations from here on Earth. One method is to look for signs of alien technology, or "technosignatures." These could come from futuristic spaceships, polluted planets, or gigantic alien construction projects. The technosignatures could be detected from light-years away and could hint at what kind of life exists elsewhere.

## DYSON SPHERE

Scientists think that advanced alien civilizations may be capable of building a device called a Dyson sphere. This gigantic structure could encircle a star, generating energy from it. Many believe that Tabby's Star is a good candidate for this technology. It occasionally dims in an irregular fashion, which could be due to a Dyson sphere. Other astronomers have argued against this however. They believe that dust clouds are responsible for the star's random dimming.

## POLLUTED PLANETS

Humans on Earth are polluting the planet. If aliens are anything like us, they might be doing the same thing. Technology can produce specific gases that are detectable from outer space, and powerful space telescopes can look at the atmospheres of planets outside the solar system to search for them. However it's important to point out that finding these gases doesn't necessarily mean that extraterrestrial life is responsible!

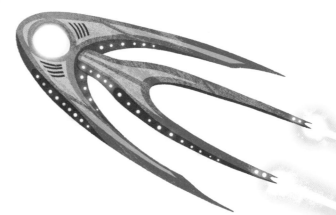

## SPACESHIPS

Advanced civilizations would need fast spaceships capable of traveling vast distances. These spaceships would be powered by a significant amount of energy, which could be detected from Earth. These signals would be different from any natural occurrences in the universe, potentially confirming that someone else is out there.

# COMET TAXIS

Comets are icy pieces of rock that hurtle through space. They may have provided Earth with the chemicals that kickstarted life. But what if they contained more than that? What if these comets carried life itself, which they deposited on Earth when they crashed into it? This theory that aliens are tranported around the universe on comets and meteors is called panspermia. Not everyone believes in it though!

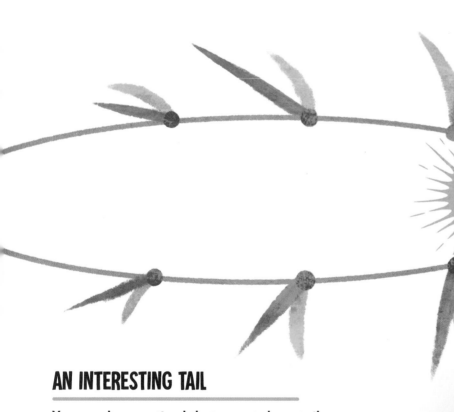

## AN INTERESTING TAIL

You may have noticed that comets have tails. You might think that these shoot out behind them as they travel through space, but that's incorrect! Comets, like planets, orbit the sun. As they get closer to it, their tails get bigger, and stream away from the heat of the star. So the tails always point away from the sun.

# FLAWS IN THE THEORY

Let's suppose that the first life-forms on Earth came from a comet impact. Why haven't they spread elsewhere? Impacts occur throughout the solar system. This means that these comets should have carried life to other places. But, as we know, we have yet to discover aliens anywhere else in the solar system. Another problem with the idea of panspermia is that more recent meteor collisions should have brought more alien life-forms to Earth—but we haven't detected any. Panspermia is a theory that leaves us with more questions than answers!

Comet      Meteor

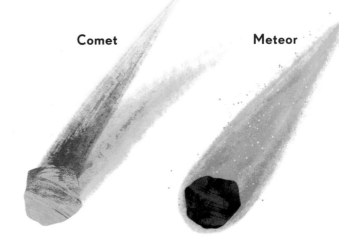

## COMETS VS. METEORS

Comets are icy rocks with tails of gas and dust trailing behind them. Meteors are pieces of rock that have entered Earth's atmosphere, also known as shooting stars.

**Tough passengers**
Not all life-forms could hitch a ride on a comet. Panspermia would require tough organisms able to withstand the extreme conditions of outer space.

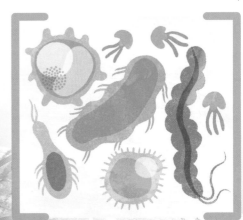

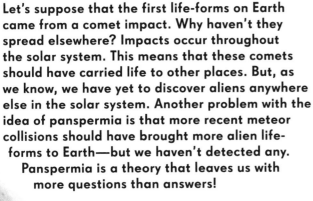

# EXOSOLAR SYSTEMS

As we peer further into our galaxy, we're finding new worlds orbiting other stars. These exosolar systems come in different shapes and sizes, and they are scattered throughout the Milky Way. The first planet orbiting a star similar to our sun was discovered in 1995, and now, almost three decades later, astronomers have found nearly 5,000 new worlds! Finding these worlds, called exoplanets, provides us with numerous candidates for places where life could exist elsewhere in the universe.

## ALIEN WORLDS

You might imagine exoplanets to be completely alien worlds. While this is true for some, many exoplanets are similar to the planets in the solar system! Some may be rocky and mountainous, while others might have lakes of water scattered across their surface. These similarities can help astronomers understand more about how exosolar systems form and the probability that they are home to alien life.

**Two stars**
Solar systems with two stars are actually pretty common!

# PLANET TYPES

Not all exoplanets are the same. Some may have a rocky surface and are capable of hosting life. Other planets could be ocean worlds or balls of icy gas like we see in our own solar system. Some planets are rogues—they don't orbit stars and just float freely across the galaxy! Planetary scientists have classified alien worlds into four general categories.

## Terrestrial
These are rocky planets similar to those in our inner solar system. They are Earth-sized or smaller and may have water on the surface and an atmosphere.

## Super Earth
This is a category exclusively based on size. These planets are much larger than Earth but smaller than Neptune. Despite their name, they aren't necessarily rocky planets like Earth.

## Neptune-like
Worlds in this category are, as you may have guessed, similar to the ice giant Neptune. They are gas planets with a rocky core.

## Gas giant
These are Jupiter-sized and bigger. They primarily have gaseous atmospheres. This category includes "hot Jupiters," which tend to orbit extremely close to their star and have scorching surface temperatures.

Powerful telescopes allow astronomers to search for planets in exosolar systems many light-years away. However, these exoplanets are small compared to stars, so they can be very hard to see. Because of this, scientists have to use different methods to find these planets and learn what they're made of. As well as exoplanets in the Milky Way, we've possibly recently discovered a planet in a whole other galaxy! Finding these far-off worlds is essential to the search for alien life. As we find more planets that could host extraterrestrial life our chances of discovering aliens increases.

## THE TRANSIT METHOD

When a planet passes in front of a star, the star's brightness dips a little bit. This is a great way to find distant exoplanets. Measuring the dip in brightness can give us information about the planet's size, distance from the star, and even its surface temperature.

The brightness dips as a planet passes in front of a star.

## OTHER METHODS

Even though scientists have found lots of exoplanets using the transit method, it does have limitations. One of them is that this process can produce a lot of false positives, meaning that not every dip in brightness is caused by a passing planet. To avoid this issue, astronomers can use other methods to try to find exoplanets.

**1**
**Wobbling stars**
A planet's gravity can cause its star to wobble a tiny bit. Scientists can detect this by measuring the star's position in the sky over time.

**2**
**Different colors**
Wobbling stars also constantly change the color of light coming from the star. If scientists spot this, they may have found a planet.

**3**
**I see you**
Although it's hard, it is possible to actually see an exoplanet! To do this, astronomers have to first find a way to block out the star's brightness.

**4**
**Magnifying glass**
A planet's gravity can focus the light shining from a star. This makes the star look temporarily brighter, meaning a planet could be nearby.

# SPACE TELESCOPES

You may not realize it, but Earth's atmosphere is constantly protecting you from harmful radiation from space. It can be annoying for astrophysicists however. They want to analyze the blocked radiation! Putting telescopes in space helps scientists get around this issue. These space observatories allow us to explore worlds outside our solar system and assist us in our search for life in the universe.

## EYES IN THE SKY

Since its launch in 1990, the Hubble Space Telescope has been completing groundbreaking scientific research in astronomy and astrobiology. Light enters the telescope, where it reflects off mirrors and is focused onto special instruments that can analyze it. Hubble has provided us with information on planets within the solar system as well as distant worlds in our galaxy.

Solar panels use light from the sun to provide Hubble with the electricity it needs to power its instruments.

The scientific instruments are housed near the front end of the telescope.

# TEAMWORK

Hubble is not alone out there. An army of telescopes in orbit around Earth have helped us in our search for life in the universe. Using these telescopes we can watch other exosolar systems forming, analyze the atmospheres on exoplanets, and much more!

### Spitzer
The Spitzer telescope looked at incoming infrared light. In order to operate, some of its instruments had to be extremely cold while others were at room temperature.

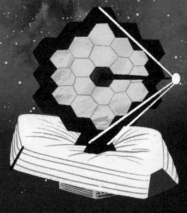

### James Webb
This telescope is meant to be Hubble's successor. It is the most powerful telescope that has been sent into space! Among other things it will search for biosignatures on exoplanets.

### TESS
TESS surveys more than 85% of the night sky for exoplanets. It uses the transit method, which looks for dips in a star's brightness over time.

### Kepler
As the predecessor to TESS, Kepler found thousands of exoplanets during its lifetime. It has discovered the most of any space telescope to date!

# NEXT-DOOR
# NEIGHBOR

Just a few light-years away sits Alpha Centauri, the closest exosolar system to us. Because of its proximity, it is a prime candidate in our search for life in the universe. To the naked eye, this star system is just a dot of light in the night sky. But as we look closer with powerful telescopes, it turns out there is more to our next-door neighbor than it seems!

Stars
A and B

## ROCKY SURFACE

The star Proxima Centauri has three planets orbiting it, designated "b," "c," and "d." Proxima Centauri b is thought to be a rocky planet with liquid on its surface that could be habitable. Planetary scientists think Proxima Centauri c is a Super Earth, possibly with rings like Saturn. Proxima Centauri d was discovered in 2022.

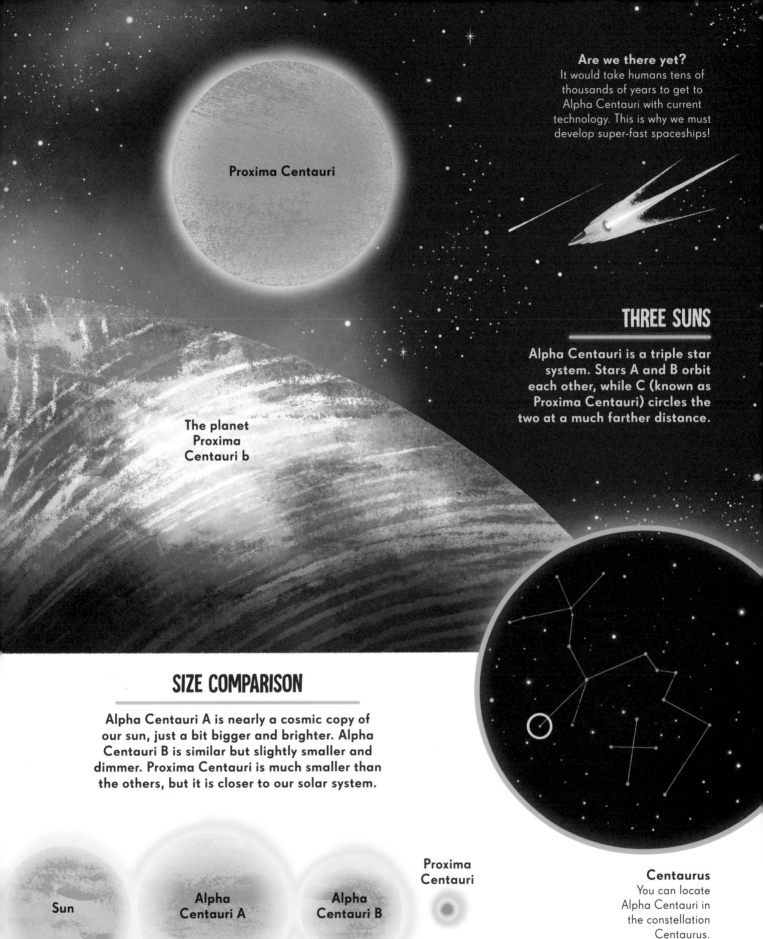

Proxima Centauri

**Are we there yet?**
It would take humans tens of thousands of years to get to Alpha Centauri with current technology. This is why we must develop super-fast spaceships!

## THREE SUNS

Alpha Centauri is a triple star system. Stars A and B orbit each other, while C (known as Proxima Centauri) circles the two at a much farther distance.

The planet Proxima Centauri b

## SIZE COMPARISON

Alpha Centauri A is nearly a cosmic copy of our sun, just a bit bigger and brighter. Alpha Centauri B is similar but slightly smaller and dimmer. Proxima Centauri is much smaller than the others, but it is closer to our solar system.

Sun

Alpha Centauri A

Alpha Centauri B

Proxima Centauri

**Centaurus**
You can locate Alpha Centauri in the constellation Centaurus.

# THE TRAPPIST-1 SYSTEM

The TRAPPIST-1 system made headlines when scientists found seven Earth-sized planets orbiting a star. Four of these planets were located in the exosolar system's habitable zone, though six of the planets may have liquid water on their surface. Scientists are incredibly excited about the TRAPPIST-1 system. It gives us a better understanding of what sort of Earth-like planets exist in our galaxy and how they could support alien life.

## ROCKY PLANETS

Scientists think that the TRAPPIST-1 planets are rocky worlds that formed a long way from their star, before moving closer to it. This exosolar system is the most studied system outside our own!

**TRAPPIST-1c**
This planet possesses a thick atmosphere similar to Venus.

**TRAPPIST-1f**
Scientists think this planet may hold more water than Earth!

**TRAPPIST-1d**
This small exoplanet sits at the edge of the system's habitable zone.

**TRAPPIST-1e**
Scientists believe this is potentially one of the most habitable planets found yet!

**TRAPPIST-1b**
This is the closest planet to the star. It takes about one and a half days to complete its orbit.

## Faraway friends

The TRAPPIST-1 system is in the constellation Aquarius. It's about 40 light-years away from us, meaning we won't be visiting anytime soon! The host star isn't visible to the naked eye and requires a powerful telescope to see it.

## Mini system

The TRAPPIST-1 exoplanets are so densely packed together that the entire exosolar system could fit inside Mercury's orbit. The planets are so close that they are clearly visible in the sky from one another. They'd appear bigger than the moon does in our sky!

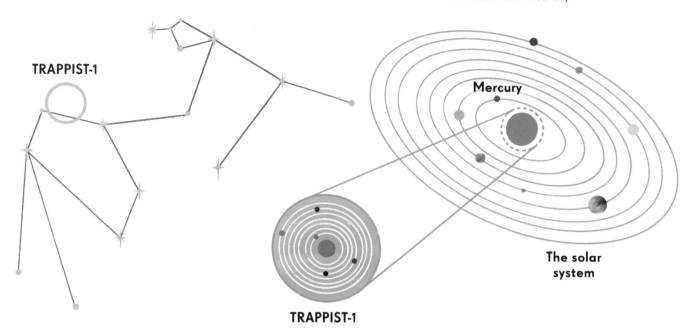

TRAPPIST-1

Mercury

The solar system

TRAPPIST-1

# PANSPERMIA

The planets are so close to one another, it opens up the possibility of panspermia occurring within the TRAPPIST-1 system. Comets and meteors may have carried alien life from planet to planet, increasing the probability of life existing here.

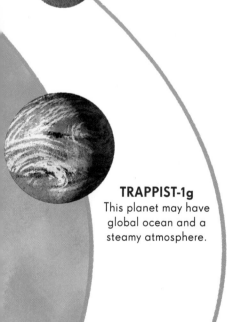

### TRAPPIST-1h
Scientists believe that this planet is too cold to host any alien life.

### TRAPPIST-1g
This planet may have global ocean and a steamy atmosphere.

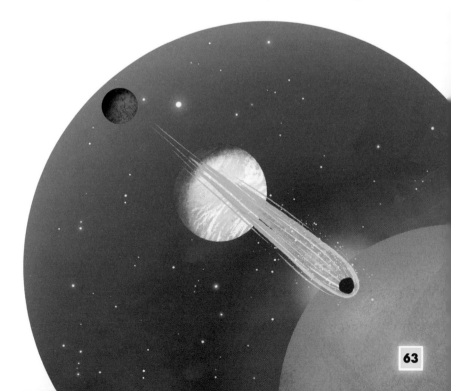

# INTERSTELLAR TRAVEL

As we look toward exosolar systems in our search for alien life, finding a way to travel to them becomes essential. The closest star (apart from the sun) is trillions of miles away, so we need to design spaceships that are fast enough to whiz us through space in a human lifetime. Interstellar travel is our only hope if we want humanity to one day orbit a star other than our own. Scientists have come up with a few ideas for how we could travel near the speed of light.

**Warp speed**
The speed of light, which is how fast light can travel in the vacuum of space, is about 186,000 miles (300,000 km) per second.

## LIGHT SAILS

Light sails would use light from a star or a laser to propel themselves forward. Using lasers is preferable, because a light sail wouldn't always be close enough to a star to get the power it needs. Since light is their fuel, light sails don't have to carry the extra weight of traditional fuels.

## INTERSTELLAR VISITOR

While interstellar spaceships are the future, we have started to spot interstellar visitors to the solar system. 'Oumuamua was the first we were aware of, speeding past in 2017. It was initially thought to be a comet, but data revealed that it didn't exhibit comet-like characteristics. Scientists think that 'Oumuamua could be the remnants of a ripped-apart planet or a whole new type of celestial object.

## ELECTRICITY

This propulsion system could create power for a spacecraft by using electricity. Though it would take longer to build up speed compared to other systems, electric propulsion could work well in combination with other methods of interstellar travel.

## NUCLEAR

Nuclear power is used to create energy on Earth, but it could also be used to power spaceships. It generates huge amounts of energy by splitting apart atoms—the tiny particles everything is made of. It would be the equivalent of setting off an atomic bomb in space!

**Grandparent**
A grandparent who was part of the initial crew will teach later generations about life on Earth.

**Parent**
Parents on these ships will have the essential responsibility of taking care of day-to-day ship duties, as well as producing and raising the next generation of inhabitants!

## HUNGRY CREW

Lots of fresh food needs to be available to keep generations of humans alive on a spaceship. Today, scientists are researching space farming, which is how to grow crops in a microgravity environment.

# GENERATION SHIPS

Super speed is one way of interstellar travel, but there is another method we could use in our search for aliens. Generation ships would be arks of people that could exist for centuries. The idea is that multiple generations of people would live on the ship to reach destinations in the universe that would take lots of time to travel to. Some of those on board may never experience what life on a planet is like! For generation ships, it is crucial to think about what is required to keep a crew alive for years to come.

**Child**
Children on these ships will be born in space and, if the destination is reached in their lifetime, could be the first to walk on an exoplanet!

## HAPPY CREW

On Earth there are lots of differences between generations, but on a generation ship it is really important that everyone is working toward the same goal. How do you ensure this if some of the crew (the younger generations) didn't sign up to the mission?

# ARE WE BEING WATCHED?

In 1950, the physicist Enrico Fermi asked his colleagues, "Where is everybody?" By everybody, he meant extraterrestrial life. If we do the math, the probability of alien life existing in the universe is significant—but humans have yet to make contact with extraterrestrials, nor have we found any relics of ancient alien civilizations. These contradictory statements give us what is called the Fermi paradox. Here are three possible ways to explain this conundrum.

## "ALIENS DON'T EXIST"

The simple answer could be that alien life does not exist elsewhere in the universe. This could be due to various reasons. Maybe very extraordinary circumstances have to take place for complex life to develop. Or maybe aliens used to exist, but they all died a long time ago. This assumption makes life on Earth feel a lot more precious!

## "INTELLIGENT LIFE EXISTS BUT IS IGNORING US"

There is a possibility that intelligent alien life does know about our existence but is avoiding making contact with humanity. They could be watching us right now! This may be because an advanced alien civilization doesn't want to interfere with Earth's evolution or accidentally contaminate our planet.

## "NON-INTELLIGENT LIFE EXISTS ELSEWHERE"

Earth is inhabited by both humans and various types of animals and plant life. Maybe life exists elsewhere in the universe, but it just isn't intelligent enough to develop advanced technology. For example, if there was an alien planet full of woodpeckers, it would make sense that they haven't yet contacted us. We'll just have to go out and find them ourselves!

# ARE WE SPECIAL?

Let's explore the idea that the conditions for complex life to evolve are super rare. When we look at how life on Earth came to be, there were lots of very specific things that had to go right. Was it just a lucky case of the right place at the right time? Or does life emerge like this frequently across the universe?

## RARE EARTH

The Rare Earth Hypothesis states it is unlikely that the conditions that created life on Earth would occur the same way elsewhere in the universe. Scientists who believe this say very simple life-forms might be present in the universe, but animal life is unique to our solar system.

# CONDITIONS FOR LIFE TO EVOLVE ON EARTH

 **Suitable galaxy**
Our galaxy is a good size and hosts a solar system in a habitable region.

 **A small star**
A smaller star, like the sun, grows slowly over time, allowing a habitable environment to develop.

 **Rocky object**
A rocky planet like Earth can hold water on its surface and retain an atmosphere.

 **Giant moon**
Our large moon stops our planet from wobbling, creating a stable environment.

 **Good timing**
Humans, an intelligent species, evolved in a period when Earth was habitable.

## ALIEN BONES

Many specific things had to go right for complex life to develop on Earth. It makes it sound unlikely that we'd ever find intelligent aliens. But you never know, one day in the future astronauts might discover bones on another planet that change everything!

# FIRST CONTACT

At some point in the future we might eventually discover aliens. What will our first contact look like? If we discover tiny microbial organisms, it may change the way we perceive the universe around us. If we encounter a more intelligent species, it might be worth making sure they know we come in peace! Coming face-to-face with aliens will make us realize that humanity isn't as unique as we thought. How do we even interact with a species so different from what we're familiar with?

## BREAKING NEWS

If we find aliens it will be headline news across the world. It will also be a mixed bag of emotions. Some people believe that we should avoid any interaction with aliens, while others think contact is essential to furthering our understanding of the cosmos. What do you think?

## TYPES OF CIVILIZATION

It might be helpful to think about the kind of societies we would encounter when making first contact. Russian astrophysicist Nikolai Kardashev tackled this issue by defining civilizations based on their technological advancements.

### Type 1 Civilization
This civilization is able to harness all of the energy and resources that exist on their home planet. Humanity has not yet reached this level.

### Type 2 Civilization
This far more advanced civilization can harness power from its host star by constructing gigantic structures such as Dyson spheres (see page 50).

### Type 3 Civilization
This futuristic civilization can harvest the power of their home galaxy, utilizing the billions of stars within it! Its inhabitants are capable of traveling between galaxies.

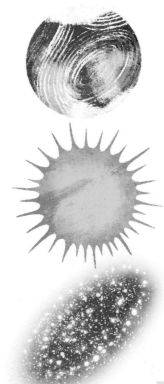

# THE FUTURE

Throughout this book we have explored many of the possible hiding spots for aliens in the cosmos. We have looked at lots of fantastic candidates that will hopefully provide us with an answer to the age-old question of whether we are alone in the universe.

Humans are a curious bunch, which means that this search for extraterrestrials will not end anytime soon. Until we have a definite answer, scientists will keep looking for aliens. That means that there is plenty of time for you (yes, you!) to get involved in astrobiology and contribute to this global effort.

You never know what awaits us out there. On a world far away, maybe on the other side of the Milky Way, might exist an alien civilization trying to figure out if they're alone as well. Hopefully one day the stars will align, and our worlds will collide!

# GLOSSARY

**ALIEN**
A creature that does not come from your planet.

**ASTEROID**
A small, rocky object that travels around a star.

**ASTROBIOLOGY**
The study of how life evolves on Earth and in the universe.

**ASTRONOMER**
A scientist who studies the universe.

**ASTROPHYSICIST**
A scientist who studies physical objects in the universe, such as stars, moons, and planets.

**ATMOSPHERE**
A layer of gases surrounding a planet or moon.

**BIOSIGNATURES**
Clues that hint at the existence of life.

**CELESTIAL BODY**
An object in outer space.

**COMET**
An icy object that travels around a star. Comets release gases when heated up.

**EVOLUTION**
The process by which living things change over different generations to adapt to the environment they live in.

**EXOPLANET**
A planet that exists outside of our home solar system.

**EXOSOLAR SYSTEM**
A solar system outside the one we live in.

**EXTRATERRESTRIAL**
A creature that does not come from Earth. Another name for an alien.

**GALAXY**
A system of stars, planets, gas, and dust held together by gravity.

**GOLDILOCKS ZONE**
The region around a star where conditions are just right for liquid water to exist on the surface of a planet.

**GRAVITY**
A force that attracts objects to each other. Gravity is what keeps you from floating off the ground!

**HABITABLE**
Able to support life.

## INTERSTELLAR OBJECT

A celestial body that exists outside of our home solar system.

## LIGHT-YEAR

The distance light can travel in one year. A light year is equivalent to 4,024,621,212,121 miles (255,000,000,000, 000,000 km)!

## METEOR

A rock from outer space that enters a planet's atmosphere.

## MICROBES

Tiny living things, or organisms.

## MILKY WAY

The galaxy that includes our home solar system.

## MOON

An object in outer space that travels around, or orbits, another object.

## ORBIT

The route an object takes when traveling around another object in outer space.

## ORGANISM

A living thing.

## PANSPERMIA

A theory stating that life is carried through space on board comets and meteors.

## PLANET

A round celestial body that orbits a star.

## PROBE

An uncrewed spacecraft sent to study a celestial body or outer space.

## SOLAR SYSTEM

A host star (or stars), planets, and other celestial objects bound together by gravity.

## TECHNOSIGNATURES

Characteristics that hint at a technologically advanced alien society.

## UFO

An unidentified flying object.

## UNIVERSE

Everything that we know to exist.

# INDEX

## This has been a
# NEON ⬙ SQUID
## production

*I'd love to dedicate this book to my entire support system: my best friend Toby Ambroise, who has been here every step of the way; my amazing close group of friends, who will always root me on; and lastly, the online space community, who have changed my life for the better.*

**Author:** Joalda Morancy
**Illustrator:** Amy Grimes
**Consultant:** Sophie Allan
**US Editor:** Allison Singer-Kushnir

## Neon Squid would like to thank:

Jane Simmonds for proofreading and Elizabeth Wise for compiling the index.

Copyright © 2022 St. Martin's Press
120 Broadway, New York, NY 10271

Created for St. Martin's Press
by Neon Squid
The Stables, 4 Crinan Street,
London, N1 9XW

EU representative: Macmillan Publishers Ireland Ltd,
1st Floor, The Liffey Trust Centre,
117–126 Sheriff Street Upper,
Dublin 1, D01 YC43

10 9 8 7 6 5 4 3 2 1

The right of Joalda Morancy to be identified as the author of this work has been asserted in accordance with the Copyright, Designs and Patents Act, 1988.

Library of Congress Cataloging-in-Publication Data is available.

Printed and bound in Guangdong, China by Leo Paper Products Ltd.

ISBN: 978-1-684-49253-4

Published in October 2022.

www.neonsquidbooks.com